By the Fireside with Dorothy

Into the Mystic

Dorothy Barklie Blandford

Published by Innisfree Spirit Ministry

South Surrey, BC, Canada

By the Fireside with Dorothy

Into the Mystic

Published by Innisfree Spirit Ministry June 2018

ISBN: 978-0-9812746-3-8

This book offers the thoughts and opinions of the author and is not to be construed in any way as a substitute for professional advice or clinical counselling.

A portion from the sale of each book will be donated to the Peace Arch Hospice Society, Surrey, BC

Dedicated to:

John Blandford

. . . for the gift of you!

Index

Thank You

No man is an island, entire of itself . . .
John Donne (1572-1631)

Neither is this compilation of whimsical stories, insights and reminiscence *an island, entire of itself,* for it has wisdom from many wise sages.

From my heart to yours . . . to my family, friends, teachers, mentors, and each one who is, or was, a part of my journey . . . *thank you!* You know who you are, and you know the journey we share is uniquely ours.

Dorothy

i

Special Recognition

For the contribution of their professional skills and gifts, I specially thank:

Andrew Grant, Personal Coach
For the countless hours of support over many years, and the ponderings that resulted in the creation of this book.

Carrie Hunter, Reverend
My Spiritual *Anam Cara (soul friend)*.

Christine Cowley, Mentor, Author and Writing Coach
For bringing flow and music to the words, and giving them space to breathe.

Eve Lees, Graphic Designer & Artistic Creator
Your skill of adapting my script into this final copy of text and illustrations is Pure Magic!

Marilyn Jamernik, Consummate Proof-reader
You were the first to read *Into The Mystic* as I held my breath, wondering if it had a life . . . your encouragement and blessing took it on its way.

Paul Bardua, Reverend, PhD
For the many threads of your gentle wisdom that are woven into the tapestry of these pages.

Valerie & Andrew Sheils, Northern Ireland
For agreeing to the cover illustration of your fireplace, beside which I spent dreamy and contented hours, and for a treasured friendship spanning many decades.

We must not cease from exploration and the result of all our exploring will be to arrive where we began and know the place for the first time.

T. S. Eliot (1888–1965)

Dear Reader . . .

*I*n the misty light of dawn, I awoke to hearing six words: *The new is in the old!* What did they mean? I had no answer, but captured them on the notepaper beside my bed. Later, much later, I believed that a clue was in the words of T. S. Eliot, which had haunted me for years by showing up randomly in reading material. While I knew there was a reason for their appearance, I had no idea what it was, until I heard those six words. The answer was not to create something new, but to look back and unveil insights from my journey.

So I have looked back at my amazing life in order to cull the highlights from almost eight decades and to share them with you. Having had a life-long fascination with words and meaningful quotations, at times I have borrowed from, and identified, beautifully expressed thoughts by wiser sages to illustrate a point.

Do you believe, as I do, that we each came to this earthly plane with a song to sing, to make a difference and to leave the world a better place with our legacy? Therein lies the

confusion as we ask: What *is* my song, how do I make a difference, what legacy can I leave? What if the life we lead *is* our legacy . . . Aah, what if . . . ?

It is also my belief that I chose my experiences before arriving on this earth. Although not understanding this in my early years, I now see how each step was, and is, a thread in a tapestry that will continue until I take my last breath and, with *Into the Mystic,* beyond.

Ireland is a land of stories and story-tellers, with the Celtic mind seeing everything as a circle. We love our tea-times and crackling fireplaces, so I've made your favourite tea, with fresh scones, and invite you to join me at the fireside as we go up hills, down valleys, and over *oops* roads, to identify the many gifts that became a thread in the tapestry of my life. Whilst there may be a generation, or more, between us, I believe many of my experiences are timeless and as relevant today as when I first encountered them, for each brought its own wisdom, albeit in hindsight.

So sip your tea and enjoy the warmth of the fire, as I weave stories that range from factual, to whimsical, to food for thought. My hope is that my hills and valleys and the stories of others I have shared, will be a light on your path and illuminate *your* amazing journey.

Blessèd be,

Dorothy Barklie Blandford
South Surrey, British Columbia, Canada
June 28, 2018

Every great dream begins with a dreamer.
Always remember, you have within you the
strength, the patience, and the passion to reach
for the stars to change the world.

Harriet Tubman (1820-1913)

Are you a Dreamer or a Dream-Maker?

Do you have whispers from your soul about something you always dreamed of doing? While remaining quietly dormant, does it still take up space in your mind? Was it too big a stretch, too far outside your comfort zone, or was your life too busy? Could you bring the dream to life again by giving it *work clothes*? The late scholar C.S. Lewis reminded us that we are never too old to set another goal or to dream a new dream. Consider scheduling some quiet time to reflect on those whispers, neither judging nor becoming daunted by their size.

Walt Disney had a plan for what he created, coining the term *imagineer*, combining imagination and engineering. He kept three chairs in his office, each one anchored to a different perspective: First, the dreamer's chair, where he visualized only the possibilities; next, the realist chair, where he defined his plan and saw the dream unfolding; then the critic's chair, to evaluate the work of the dreamer and realist and find a win-win solution. This is a capsule version of the principle he and his many *imagineers* applied for each idea. Today we continue to be inspired by the Disney legacy.

Some dreams present themselves and then lie buried until resurrected, but never forgotten. In my 40s the seed of Hospice was planted, which lay dormant for 20 years before my busy life quietened and I became a volunteer, ultimately leading to a ministry focus of compassionate care. In my 50s I heard an inner voice saying I would become a minister, and immediately responded: *Not me, God, NO way*! At 70, now a minister, the voice again whispered that I embark on studies leading to a PhD in Metaphysics. Outrageous, I thought! Yet, step by tiny step, each one came about, despite my doubts along the way. I did not do it alone, but received support from many wise teachers.

Not all of our dreams come to fruition, even when we have a logical *why*. In my 30s, I enrolled in a car mechanics course for women, thinking I *should* know something about how the engine worked. Back at home my frustrated partner twisted paper clips to illustrate how the carburetor turned! Ultimately, I decided to service my car regularly, trust that when I turned the ignition key it would start, and I didn't need to know the *why* or the *how*! There is a time to let go, and a time to revisit.

Have you dreams tucked away that could be dusted off and brought to light for consideration, open to the possibility of their achievement? Michelangelo once said that the greatest danger for most of us is not that our aim is too high and we miss it, but that our aim is actually too low and we reach it. As children, we are great dreamers. It is never too late to become a dream-maker by revisiting the life you once envisioned, in its original or modified form, or with new ideas. And you don't have to do it alone!

Happy *Imagineering!*

In my walks, every man I meet is my superior
in some way, and in that I learn from him.
Ralph Waldo Emerson (1803-1882)

Connections

*I*have had a lifelong interest in meaningful quotations, many of which have been pasted into journals. The one I shared by Emerson was the start of that interest, and spoke to me in ways that became clearer during various stages of my life, where each provided a snippet of great wisdom or a valuable life lesson. Some of my lessons came from formal teachers, others during countless workshops, brief conversations in a bookstore, a restaurant, during a journey, or from a book *just happening* to fall off a shelf and opening to the information I needed.

Would you agree that synchronicity is very powerful, and seldom a coincidence? One never forgotten lesson was a *chance* meeting with a young girl during a sacred pilgrimage to Ireland, while standing on a street corner in Galway. As she saw life, we were all a piece of a beautiful mosaic, and without each one of us it would not be complete. What a beautiful connection!

Another person who presented an insightful life connection metaphor was a fellow student during a writing course, where our final assignment was to write about a ball of yarn that had taken on a life of its own. With her permission I reproduce it below.

Explaining how we relate to one another has been attempted by many, but only vaguely accomplished by a few. The connection of human spirit is both obvious and elusive and when contained by words the outcome appears somehow diminished. Metaphor is perhaps the best we can do to produce a picture that captures the essence of our relationship to one another.

Imagine as you navigate through life that you leave a trail of yarn in your path. The yarn is your past, your present, and will follow you into your future. Everyone else also leaves a trail of yarn in their path. As these millions of threads meander with life they may touch each other. Consider how many people you encounter in a single day and the dozens, perhaps hundreds of occasions where your thread touches another. First impression is one of a huge tangle of yarn that may create a chaotic ball of paralysis.

Life means growth, and with growth our yarn continues to spin and move forward despite occasional knots and tangles. With each touch of a strand energy is shared, consciously or not. As one strand touches another a relationship is formed, for a second, a moment, or a lifetime. We are each uniquely changed by the touching of our yarns.

— *Leslie Konkin, Dec. 2009, used with permission.*

Reflecting on your life with its many connections, can you see how the synchronicity of your *threads of yarn* coming together was not a coincidence, and how in some way you were uniquely changed? Let's continue to be open to the rich revelations and insights of our many teachers . . . remembering we are each a piece of a beautiful mosaic!

You are, at this moment, standing right in the middle of your own acres of diamonds.

Earl Nightingale (1921-1989)

Young Loves

Those young loves that shaped the path we travelled and became life-defining. The three I share took place between the ages of 11 and 14, with two remaining among my *acres of diamonds*, and a third that shattered my heart into a million pieces.

First love, age 11: Attending public school was mandatory, but not exciting until *domestic science*, a weekly cooking class, was added. Ingredients were carried in a basket covered with a white linen serviette, along with a freshly washed and ironed apron made the previous year. This began my love affair with cooking and weekly home baking . . . when combining the margarine (butter was then rationed) and sugar was done with a wooden spoon in a yellow bowl, first set by the hearth to soften and hasten the mixing. Over the years electric mixers and modern appliances replaced the wooden spoon, but the love of recipes, cookbooks and cooking classes has never lost its magic. This also started my love affair with lists, as grocery shopping became my role.

Next love, age 14: By way of total disclosure, I got caught playing hooky at a prior secondary school, after which my father sternly asked: *Madam, what are you doing with your life, what do you want to do?* '*Madam*' meant I was in trouble and he was serious! *Learn typing, shorthand, and get a job,* I replied. Thankfully, my parents agreed. True bliss was walking into that first typing class to the deafening roar of 20 Underwood manual typewriters, and learning to touch-type with a box over the keys – which I now appreciate. Pitman's shorthand was a joy, as I could capture words of favourite songs (and still do)! The two years at Business College became the solid foundation for the rest of my life, and led to my first office job at a college, and ongoing night classes. Brad Henry, former Governor of Oklahoma, believed *a good teacher inspired hope, ignited imagination and instilled a love of learning.* I am still learning.

Life shattering love, age 14: Thrilled when red-haired John asked to walk me home after church, I assured my mother our friendship would last forever. Gently, she agreed that it could, but didn't always. My great romance lasted a matter of weeks, during which I learned to distinguish different car models and received my first boy-girl kiss, before being told it was over – the reason long forgotten. At 14, I was shattered and heart-broken. Reproducing this story brought up a long forgotten memory of sobbing out the sad tale to my elocution teacher – echoing the late Maya Angelou's belief, that the loss of young first love is so painful that it borders on the ludicrous! Was I ever *so* young?

Did my reflections trigger thoughts of your significant young loves? Did they bring warm smiles? Did any painful memories remind you how resilient you were, and are? Let's bridge the years from where we were to where we are, with appreciation for today's gifts and the journey we've taken. I certainly am grateful for current technology and its many conveniences . . . for a speedy food processor instead of laborious mixing with a wooden spoon, my computer's vast research capabilities, and for central heating. To this day I remain an avid list-maker, and wear an apron when cooking.

I leave you to reminisce about your young loves and those that continue to be among your *acres of diamonds.*

Memories are special moments that tell our story.

Anonymous

Memories

When operating an office services company in Victoria, British Columbia, I received wise advice from a client about the value of creating memories, so that later in life I could smile as I turned the pages of my Memory Book. I believe that reminiscing about special times is like being wrapped up in a cosy blanket while sitting in front of a crackling fire on a frosty morning. The *crackling fire* may need to be replaced by a gas or electric fireplace, the Christmas log on television, or musings at the beach . . . but, you get my drift!

What are your cherished memories? Do they bring smiles, sadness or tears? After the loss of a special person, or a broken relationship, we may think the shattered pieces of our heart will never mend. Yet, tears and time are great healers.

In your early years did you long to be older – 16, 18, or 21! When my father told me that after 21 the years would escalate faster than ever, I didn't believe him . . . mmmh, how right he was! From where I am now my memories are certainly lengthy, seeming that I've lived many lifetimes during my years. In the forties the lamplighter came along on his bicycle each evening outside my window, climbing the lamp post to light the mantle; at Christmas time, when relatives gathered in my grandmother's small cottage, my sister, cousins and I would 'primp' in readiness for Christmas dinner, each year feeling more 'grown-up'; going to the dance hall on a Saturday evening where boys lined up on one side and girls on the other – praying a brave boy would cross the floor and ask us to dance!

Among my richest memories are those of listening to stories from people in their eighties and nineties, who knew what it was like to live with very little. My late husband was interviewed by Canadian author, Robert Collins for his book, *You Had To Be There*. It contains interviews with 181 men and women who had experienced the Depression and World War II years. Woven throughout is a definition of happiness that was a sign of the times:

> *We are the last link to a remarkable almost mythic time . . . we have lived through monumental change . . . from horse-and-buggy, Model-T Ford, to crank-handle telephone, to moon walks, space shuttles, and the Internet . . . we laughed ourselves silly . . . we were so poor and didn't know it. And we had so much fun, 'cause we shared. And we looked after each other.*

Memories remain one of life's precious gifts, especially during birthdays, anniversaries, significant sacred times, or when looking back at photographs. From wherever you are on your journey, continue to create rich experiences, and share the treasured memories you made, for they tell your amazing story.

A friend is a gift you give yourself.
Robert Louis Stevenson (1850-1894)

Odd Couple Friendships

An odd couple, would you say? The small lamb bought in a village in Ireland with a *Love* tag, supporting a smiling cow made by a friend. They bring to mind, when living on 100 acres in Ontario, how my English bulldog, Paddy, made friendship overtures to the cows grazing in the field. Paddy thought everyone was her friend, and wiggled with joy when smiling passersby stopped to admire her.

Do you have favourite *odd couple* inspirational stories that speak to you, fact or fiction? One of mine is in the children's book *Charlotte's Web* by E.B. White, where a spider (Charlotte) weaves words in her web and saves a piglet (Wilbur), who asks her why she did it. *You have been my friend; that itself is a tremendous thing,* said Charlotte.

A *tremendous thing* is the true story of courage, survival and healing about a scruffy little dog with short legs that changed a man's life in a positive way. Dion Leonard was running his seventh ultra-marathon through the Gobi Desert – a self-sufficiency week of 250 kilometers over grueling conditions in extreme heat – when he was joined by the little dog. Despite his determination to win the race, he stopped to help her across deep water and share his meager rations. Later, after overcoming huge hurdles, he brought her to his home in Scotland, appropriately naming her *Gobi*. His book, *Finding Gobi,* is a stirring and heartwarming story.

During our lifetime we experience a mixture of emotions due to changing circumstances. Some are peaceful and others traumatizing, spinning us into a whirlwind of angst that forces us to dig deeply for inner strength, often taking us in a new direction.

Like the seasons, friendships can change over time, but as we are the one person who will be with us our entire lifetime, the greatest gift we can give ourselves is to be our own best friend. As *Charlotte* said to *Wilbur, that itself is a tremendous thing!*

None of us knows what might happen even the next minute, yet still we go forward. Because we trust. Because we have faith.

Paulo Coelho (from novel, Brida)

Reluctant Feline Owner

Recalling a favourite movie of the late fifties, *The Reluctant Debutante,* starring Kay Kendall and Rex Harrison, I could play the lead role in a production of *The Reluctant Feline Owner.* Here's my story!

While attending an SPCA Annual General Meeting, I learned that a bedraggled three-legged calico cat, *Carmelle,* had recently arrived, about to have kittens, and been placed with a caring foster volunteer so as to have her family in comfort. During the next two months, despite a busy schedule, this calico cat occupied a part of my mind. Following up, I learned that five healthy kittens had gone to new homes, *Carmelle* spayed, and was now available for adoption.

Did I immediately make a decision to adopt her? No!!! One day I would, the next day I had many reasons not to . . . I was then 69, what if she lived for 20 years, what if there were major veterinarian bills and I couldn't pay them . . . etc., etc. Following the sudden death of my husband in December 2003, I had considered adopting a cat or fostering one, but there was always a reason to delay: studying . . . writing exams . . . an overseas trip, to name a few.

Then fate stepped in – divine intervention – when I was asked if I would care for *Carmelle* during the weekend, as her foster-mother was going out of town. I agreed. On Friday, Saturday, Sunday, we enjoyed each other's company. She ate her food, used a scratching post, her litter box, and made herself at home. Sunday evening, as I picked up the phone to arrange her return, I burst into tears!!! What in the world was going on?!!!

Explaining that I had no idea why the tears, and was still undecided about adopting her, I heard the laughing response: *I know what's wrong with you . . . you're in love*!!! Oh, Goodness!!! We decided I would keep *Carmelle* for another night and discuss the matter next day with the SPCA, when it was agreed that I would keep her until I made a decision, or she was adopted, whichever came first.

A couple of mornings later, still indecisive and tearful, while standing at my kitchen counter, the reason thundered into my mind: *I didn't want to need her*! On the heels of that were words from the 1993 movie, *Shadowlands,* starring Anthony Hopkins and Debra Winger: *The pain then is part of the happiness now.* Suddenly, there was no hesitation; it was a matter of trusting, having faith and making the commitment. Next day, with adoption arrangements finalized, I renamed her *Cadi*, an Irish name meaning *simple happiness*.

Cadi knows how to be *in the moment.* She eats, sleeps, looks out on her world from various windows, and decides when to do each, including getting what she wants when she wants it, a skill she has perfected over the past ten years. Yes, we continue to have traumas, such as getting her into a pet carrier to visit her veterinarian, a nerve-racking experience for both of us, as she makes her displeasure loudly heard on the journey – until she is transferred into his care, when she is a paragon of angelhood!

As I wrote at the beginning in *Dear Reader,* I believe our lives are like a tapestry, with threads connecting us to each person and experience, in perfect timing. Knowing I had an out-of-town trip later in the year, I did a search to find someone who provided in-home care, and learned of Grace McGran (www.petgranny.com)*. Serendipitously, her husband, Noel,* had just taken early retirement and was planning to provide website support, which I also needed. We journeyed together for nine years during which Noel, also from Ireland, enhanced *Innisfree's* website with its Celtic image and newsletter illustrations, until his sudden death.

It is now ten years since *Cadi* came into my life. Am I glad I made the decision to adopt her? Yes, without a doubt, despite initial anxiety about having one day to let her go. Grief due to loss is painful and challenging, yet hopefully balanced with happy memories. *To live in hearts we leave behind is not to die,* wrote Scottish poet, Thomas Campbell (1777-1844).

*Names used with permission. The February 2017 Innisfree Moment on New Beginnings is dedicated to Noel and may be found at http://www.innisfreespirit.com/moment.php?n=1

Listen contains the same letters as silent.

Alfred Brendel, Austrian pianist, poet and author.

Listening to the Whispers of Your Heart

Going into the silence and listening to the whispers of our heart can provide intuitive answers that become absolute truths. I share the following true story:

My Friend, Flo, Black Cocker Spaniel:

It was in Northern Ireland, mid-1940s, that a five-year-old girl sat in a stable on a bed of straw. Billy, the horse that pulled the open trap that transported her grandparents into the near-by town, stood in his stall, watching the girl with her arm around the black cocker spaniel, Flo. Hours went by, but time stood still! At some point her grandmother came in and covered them both with fresh straw for warmth, and to this day she remembers its sweet smell. As twilight was closing in, she was brought into the house where the oil lamps were already lit for the evening. She never saw Flo again.

More than 70 years later, reflecting on the experience, the girl knew that Flo was dying. Over the years, at significant times, that inner intuitive sense would serve her well. I was that girl.

While I spent a great portion of my life multi-tasking at a frenetic pace, I now trust that when I become silent, surrender and ask for an answer – and really listen – it will be provided, as it was over a recent move, when considering returning to Victoria, BC on Vancouver Island, where I had lived previously. I had sold my home but was undecided about the wisdom of the more major move from the mainland.

After looking at apartments, none of which felt right, early the next morning I walked to the fountain at Victoria's Beacon Hill Park, and while listening to the waterfall and watching the meandering ducks on the path, clearly heard "no," followed by a softer "not now." With my mind at rest, I returned to the mainland and soon found an ideal apartment in the area of my alternative choice. With hindsight, it was the better choice, even though Victoria will always hold a piece of my heart. Only when I surrendered and trusted, was the answer provided. Whether I ever return to live will be a decision made at that time. (The chapter *Stepping Stones* has a segment on *Surrender*).

In our busy world the greatest gift we can give ourselves, especially if confused, is to stop and listen in the silence.

The greatest gift we can give another is to listen deeply, without judgment, resisting the temptation to jump in quickly with our opinion, sure we have the answer. Noted hymn-writer and theologian, Frederick William Faber put it wisely: *As well as the grace of kind speaking there is also the grace of kind listening.* In meeting with others who have a weight on their mind, I often find they just need me to listen, so they can hear their own truth.

In the quiet, what whispers have you heard? Did you heed them?

Courage does not always roar. Sometimes it is a quiet voice at the end of the day saying: 'I will try again tomorrow.'
Mary Anne Radmacher, Artist and Author

It takes Courage to be Courageous

C an you recall a time when you were very brave despite terror in your heart? One of my courageous steps was when, in my mid-teens and first job in a typing pool at a College in Belfast, an opportunity arose to become secretary to one of the headmasters. Knowing it was an important next step on my career path, after a sleepless night and with shaking knees, I asked to be considered – this was in the mid-fifties when bosses were revered and put on a pedestal! Yes, I did get the position, and learned that I would not have been considered, as my supervisor didn't think I would be interested.

It was a valuable lesson that I have applied throughout my life, that if we don't ask, the answer is always "no"! When overwhelmed, a courageous step can be asking another for support. Working with a personal coach, as I continue to do, allows us to hear what we think, and get another's input for consideration. Lance Secretan, in his book *One* wrote:

Courage is not the absence of fear but rather the judgment that something else is more important than fear.

It can take courage to say "no" and not go along with the crowd. Not having that courage can provide valuable lessons, albeit harsh ones, as I learned. As the only dissenter of a decision to strike, I was asked in a crowded room by the emcee (a close friend), "Dorothy, are you with us?" Reluctantly, I agreed. At the end of the meeting a beautiful gentle soul said she was undecided but encouraged when I agreed. I felt ill, as I knew that I did not agree, but had gone along with the crowd and not been authentically true to myself. Some years later I discovered *Creativity,* by Alan Ashley Pitt: *The man who follows the crowd will usually get no further than the crowd . . . You have two choices in life; you can dissolve into the mainstream, or you can be distinct. To be distinct, you must be different. To be different, you must strive to be what no one else but you can be.* That verse remains in a prominent place in my home, as a reminder of a harsh but valuable life lesson.

Have you been inspired by the music of the iconic Elvis Presley? I read that he was turned down by his school's Glee Club because he didn't conform to their style of music. What joy we would have missed if he had said to himself, "Guess they're right" and chosen another career path. It takes courage to step forward and move out of the shadows, especially if you were taught to conform.

Have you been keeping yourself small and hiding behind a mask? Have the courage to ask and answer those questions. But also be kind to yourself if, with hindsight, you wish you had made another decision. You did the best you could at the time. Instead, replace that hindsight wish with acknowledgment for a time when you were brave. It takes courage to be courageous and, as Mary Anne Radmacher wrote, it does not always roar, but can be a quiet voice.

Keep all special thoughts and memories for lifetimes to come. Share these keepsakes with others to inspire hope and build from the past, which can bridge to the future.
Mattie J.T. Stepanek (1990-2004)

Keepsake Medallion

What if you were gifted a keepsake medallion, inscribed with letters representing the strengths that someone saw in you? What would the letters represent and, more important, would you own what they represented?

I was given such a gift for my 45th birthday by my late husband, subsequent to a business offer that embodied a major vision I had set for this date ten years prior. It was a gold disc with my initials, the date, and the letters A-B-C-D-E-F-G, representing Ambition – Bravery – Confidence – Dedication – Enterprise – Faith – Guts, later adding "S" for Spirit and Spirituality. For thirty-four years I have worn it each day, as an inspirational token. Did I initially 'own' the words? No, especially B and C. I continued to second-guess myself, 'dying a thousand deaths' as I pushed my comfort zone to its limits, or compared myself to someone more talented. Then gradually, ever so gradually, I honoured times when I was brave, and when I had confidence. With hindsight, brave steps were immigrating to Canada with two suitcases and $40 in the sixties, representing myself in divorce proceedings in the seventies, starting an office services company in the eighties, and now, three decades later, continuing to push my comfort zone by writing this book!

Wherever you are on your journey, take reflective time to identify and honour your strengths and gifts, for they are uniquely yours. Marianne Williamson reminds us with her often-quoted words, that our playing small does not serve the world. The world wants and needs our gifts. So your mission, if you choose to accept it, is to ask a trusted source for input, design your keepsake medallion, and share its significance with your world!

The quotation for this section is in the words of Mattie Stepanek, the young boy who had a rare form of muscular dystrophy, but in his short life was known as a peace advocate, inspiring the world with his essays. He knew he had a mission, and so do we!

The only limits you have are the limits you believe.
Wayne D. Dyer (1940-2015)

Labels Limit

Some years back, during a *Women in Business* networking meeting in Vancouver, I met a creative girl who had recently been a principal dancer with the Royal Ballet of London and was then writing poetry. We had like-minded discussions until our paths moved in different directions but, before leaving she gifted me with some words in beautiful script that are as meaningful today as back then:

> *To find inner peace, let go of your identity. Say to yourself, I am 'me,' nothing else matters. Don't limit yourself by saying who you are professionally, or only this, or only that. Think of all the many different things you could do, if you had no labels. Remember, 'labels limit.'*

Do you ever label yourself with what you believe is your truth, so it stops you from attempting something you would like to do? Would you be willing to change that belief? A sad parable is about an eagle that never soared because it believed it was a chicken. Paraphrasing, the story is about a man who found an eagle's egg and placed it under a brooding hen. The eaglet hatched with the chickens and grew to be like them. Years pass and the eagle, now grown old, sees a magnificent bird above him in the sky, gliding with scarcely a movement of its golden wings. Spellbound, the eagle asked, "Who's that?" "That's the king of the birds, the eagle," said his neighbour. "Wouldn't it be wonderful if we could soar like that," said the eagle. "Don't give it another thought, we're chickens, he belongs to the sky, we belong to the earth." So the eagle lived and died a chicken, for that's what he thought he was. (*The Golden Eagle,* from *The Song of the Bird,* by Anthony de Mello).

In an opposite vein, someone who did not put labels on herself is Roz Savage, who at 36 made a solo trip across the Atlantic in a rowboat, a feat that few of us would even think of attempting. Being stuck in a job rut and an unravelling marriage, she wrote two versions of her obituary – one if she continued the *normalcy* of her present life, and the other if she lived the life she dreamed. She chose the latter! In a Vancouver television interview she admitted that her 3,000 mile sea journey was very challenging, but she knew why she was doing it, epitomizing Nietzsche's words, "He who has a *why* to live for can bear almost any *how*." Her inspiring book is *Rowing the Atlantic – Lessons Learned on the Open Ocean.*

What personal message can we take from these stories that emphasize the power of our thoughts and beliefs? Let's not regret what didn't come to pass, but be grateful for the choices we made. No, I didn't attempt my pilot's licence, or purchase the spiffy MG sports car I fell in love with, but I did other amazing things, and I know you did too. So acknowledge your accomplishments, and use them as a springboard for going forward. Just write two versions of your obituary, know your *why*, break it down into small steps, and believe in yourself . . . without any limiting labels! That's how I came to finish writing my PhD dissertation, which almost didn't get done!

*In the sweetness of friendship let there be laughter,
and sharing of pleasures. For in the dew of little
things the heart finds its morning and is refreshed.*

Kahlil Gibran (1883-1931)

Laughter and Smiles

*D*id you laugh today? Did you smile? We read about the healing benefit of laughter, how it relaxes tense muscles and reduces stress. As children, we used to laugh hundreds of times a day, but often less as adults. If we live alone, we can go too long without laughter, or even smiles, and take ourselves too seriously. A Norwegian study found that laughter can help us live longer, and that even if we had a humourless childhood we can learn to embrace the absurdity of life at any age. https://www.scientificamerican.com/article/laugh-lots-live-longer

Smiles are contagious, and giving one of yours can result in one being returned, such as a connection at the grocery checkout, or on an elevator. Most people like to be asked to help and with my five foot height, needing assistance for a top shelf unreachable item is often followed by a warm exchange.

Research indicates that sharing a laugh with another has great mutual value. I had a friend in her nineties to whom I read bedtime stories twice a week by phone, once she got tucked into bed at her care residence. We always laughed together – sometimes about the antics of my 3-legged cat who liked to 'plop down' on the page I was reading from an inspirational story, or a favourite fairy story, proving the wisdom of the late C.S. Lewis of Narnia books fame: *Some day you will be old enough to start reading fairy tales again.* Our last time together was a few hours before she died, so perhaps the happy memories eased her transition.

Is your home happy? Do you feel contentment when you enter? Do you see meaningful mementoes, a cartoon, an uplifting saying? One of my walls has the large "Laugh" sculpture illustrated and three plaques in Ogham – an ancient Irish 1st century alphabet – representing Peace, Tranquility and Happiness. How about creating a laughter kit to open when you have been taking yourself too seriously? Mine contains numerous silly and outrageous items sent by like-minded friends, which I also take to workshop presentations. It certainly creates laughter! What would you put into yours?

The first 10 seconds of each morning set an important tone for the day. Birds know this and can be heard singing while it's still dark. Whatever warms your heart creates an inner smile, and a smile is the beginning of a laugh. American football coach, Duff Daugherty, felt we only needed three bones to journey successfully through life: A wishbone to dream with, a backbone for courage to get through the hard times, and a funny bone to laugh at life along the way.

I wish you smiles and laughter on your journey.

Correction does much, but encouragement does more.
Johann Wolfgang von Goethe (1749-1832)

Communicating with Kindness

The art of kind communication is priceless. When delivered in a considerate way it can strengthen a relationship; when not, it can demolish, as do misunderstandings that remain unsaid. Initiating a conversation is challenging for many of us, and easy to avoid, especially when there is a perceived risk of disagreement. A good friend was upset with something her husband did, and responded to my question of whether they had discussed the matter with an adamant, *he knows*! Much later, she realized he had had no idea, and could have avoided carrying the weight of injured feelings by 'putting it on the table' at the time. Again, not always easy to do!

Communication is the invaluable training component of Toastmaster membership. Recently receiving an anniversary invitation from a local Club to which I had belonged, my thoughts drifted to personal experiences with previous Clubs over the years . . . it was the best of times, and the worst of times! Best was listening to interesting topics from fellow members; worst was lengthy preparation and delivery of speeches, with greatest anxiety when in the role of evaluator; yet, also the best, as I learned to apply kindness with the *sandwich formula:* Compliment (acknowledge the speaker's efforts) – Critique (with helpful suggestions) – Compliment (conclude with encouragement), using first person phrasing. It is a formula fitting for many of life's communicative situations, especially when combined with *kind listening* – a term used by hymn-writer, F.W. Faber and also referenced in the chapter *Listening to the Whispers of Your Heart.*

Depending on the year / culture, our teachers and parents may have emphasized how we could have done better, without acknowledging the effort we put into a project. Although at times mine did, I can now accept it was their way of motivating me to attain higher standards. While that was then, today do we continue to hear and act on that critical voice? If so, a recent email from Robert Holden contained an ideal remedy. He suggested checking whether the voice we listened to was our inner critic or our inner coach. Our inner critic sends a negative message – no way, can't do it, not good enough; whereas our inner coach is our "yes" energy – a much kinder, loving and encouraging voice. Holden is the author of *Success Intelligence* and director of *The Happiness Project*; his newsletters can be subscribed to at www.robertholden.com

Mother Teresa reminds us that kind words can be short and easy to speak, but their echoes are endless. So let's communicate kindly with ourselves, and encourage the efforts of others by first putting ourselves in their shoes . . . which need not be ours! Those echoes may reverberate far and wide and inspire others!

Have you been stopped by listening to your inner critic? What would your inner coach encourage you to do?

*I believe that a part of our mind foresees the
entire course of a relationship before we begin it,
and we choose to enter that series of events as the
gentlest possible way to learn the lessons we are
now ready to learn.*

Hugh Prather (1938-2010)

Joining me on my Bench of Dreams

. . . A Special Person

You have a relaxing favourite seat in Nature that is your *Bench of Dreams*, and where at times you invite significant people to join you. Today you are meeting for the first time someone who has been your inspiration. It is a warm spring day with the sun shining through the gentle breeze of the trees as you anticipate the arrival of this special person. Who is joining you? Why have you chosen this person?

I have chosen the late Irish poet, author, mystic, former priest, John O'Donohue (1956-2008), who was born on a farm and continued to live in the wild Connemara region of Western Ireland known as The Burren. As he walks towards me I breathe a sigh of contentment, knowing our experience will be a *time out of time,* with much shared laughter and wisdom, and listening as he reads his poetry.

Why did I choose him? *John was comfortable in his own skin,* said an early school friend and shopkeeper that I met during a pilgrimage to Ireland in the village of Ballyvaughan on Galway Bay. I was inspired when hearing him being interviewed during an earlier visit to Vancouver, BC, and had hoped to join one of the groups he invited to his home, but he died suddenly at 52. During the pilgrimage we stopped at Creggagh Cemetery to share some *holy water* (Irish Whiskey), before sprinkling the balance on his gravesite! John loved his whiskey! He also knew what was important in his life and, after 19 years left the priesthood to pursue his hankering to write. His first book, *Anam Cara* (soul friend) is an insightful one, from which I learn something new each time I open it.

A more important reason I chose this wise teacher is that his books and talks helped me clarify what I most wanted to accomplish during my lifetime and that, even if I didn't do everything the best way, I'd give it my best shot.

So that's who I chose to join me on my *Bench of Dreams*. In the midst of our sharing and laughter there were times of comfortable silence. Later, we sauntered along to a local pub for some Irish Whiskey while continuing to chat, bringing to an end a perfect day! https://www. johnodonohue.com

I invite you to sit on your *Bench of Dreams* and reflect on the special person you chose to join you. Did what you shared together lead to making an important shift in your thinking?

I am tomorrow, or some future day, what I establish today. I am today what I established yesterday, or some previous day.

James Joyce (1882-1941)

. . . My Younger Self

On this perfect summer's day you have returned to your favourite *Bench of Dreams*. Smiling, you stand to welcome the young person walking towards you . . . your younger self. On this visit you share wisdom that took you many years to acquire. I am meeting my 16 year-old self, the year I commenced full-time employment. At the end of our time together, I hand her a personal letter with this message:

There is so much I could share with you from my many years of living; in part, to save you from going down the 'oops' roads that I did. But, you will live your life and create your own path. So I have chosen only my most significant for you to contemplate.

Wake each day with gratitude, for you have come through the night and been presented with a bank account of 1,440 minutes, which can only be used but never reclaimed.

Dare to dream . . . your dreams may become your destiny.

Create a balanced lifestyle. Your career, travel time and

*continuous learning will take up many hours, but always nurture
your family and friendships, your faith, and your health.*

*You will be tested with challenges that will make you stronger.
They may not be what you wanted, but be exactly what you
most needed to lead you to your next experience.*

Be in service to others, in whatever way speaks to your heart.

*Take time to be alone with yourself, to reflect, enjoy music,
reading and the outdoors.*

*Listen to the young and the older, for each can be your teacher.
Really listening, without judgment, is the greatest gift you can offer.*

Laugh often; remain young at heart and curious about life. In the
words of one *of the greatest minds in history, Albert Einstein: "I
have no special talent, I am only passionately curious."*

*You will receive wisdom from many sources. Ultimately, the
answers you seek are within your heart, and were there all the time
just waiting for your discovery. Legendary country singer, Dolly
Parton, said it best: "Find out who you are and do it on purpose."*

I urge you, my younger self, with every beat of your heart and
every breath you take, to be grateful for the gift of you, for each
day and what it brings, and each one on your journey. Have a
beautiful life.

What are the wise insights in your mind, just waiting, and
wanting, to be shared with *your* younger self?

The future is something which everyone reaches at the rate of 60 minutes an hour, whatever he does, whoever he is.

C.S. Lewis (1898–1963)

. . . My Future Self

Returning to your *Bench of Dreams* on this autumn day, with the sun shining and birds singing, your feet having crunched on the crisp coloured leaves, you await the arrival of today's special guest . . . your 20-year-older future self. You will have the opportunity to ask some questions about which you are curious. My future self has just celebrated her 100th birthday. Here is our – at times humorous – question and answer exchange:

Q. How did you celebrate your birthday?

A. With style, wearing my brightest colours, and listening to my favourite music – Strauss waltzes and Irish favourites – and afternoon tea, with cream scones!

Q. Do you feel you are 100?

A. I don't know what 100 is supposed to feel like. Some days I don't feel any age, and when my memory shifts to an earlier occasion or I look at photographs, I see myself at that age, as if the years have flowed seamlessly . . . and so swiftly!

Q. Do you have regrets, or things that you wish you could change?
A. No. I used to think, in hindsight, I'd have been smarter to do this or that, but if I had, the journey I took would be different . . . and I had – am still having – an amazing life, meeting interesting people. If I'd made other decisions I would have missed out on what I did.

Q. Are you afraid to die?
A. No. I hope it will be a good death, with dignity, and be in a room with a view, looking out at the ocean and the trees, just like the picture on my wall. I feel I've lived many lifetimes during my years, and where I'm going next will be a new 'schoolroom' where I'll keep learning . . . and meeting old friends! Mmmh, wonder what we'll get up to? That's not for today, and today is a good day!

Q. What wisdom would you offer for my next 20 years?
A. Be the star in your own life, and maybe a tad outrageous . . . you've earned the right! Don't take yourself too seriously, nor isolate yourself, nor *act your age,* whatever that means! Listen to your favourite music. Laugh a lot, and cry when something touches you, or during a sad movie. Marvel at something every day. As long as you are able, keep active and involved . . . consider it part of your DNA! And all those memories you made . . . enjoy visiting them, but don't build a condominium and live in them . . . that was an expression a wise minister teacher liked to remind his

students. And you want to know what keeps me young . . . my daily medicinal Irish Whiskey!

Q   WOW! Good advice. Thank you.

A.   Now, off you go and write yourself a letter, to *your* 100-year-old self!

What chronological age is your future self? What wonderful wisdom did you share? Will you heed it? How?

Live
Simply.

*Life is really simple, but we insist
on making it complicated.*

Confucius.

Simplicity! Just let me lead a simple life . . . with no clutter!

Just let me lead a simple life . . . with no clutter, is our desperate prayer. Few things are as overwhelming as clutter. Among other things it includes paper, clothes, furnishings, quotations, cards, unfinished projects and emails . . . all taking up energy! Deciding what items to keep, and what not, can be daunting. Logically, we know order doesn't happen unless we take action, and action might mean putting a buddy system of support in place. And . . . no way around it . . . it takes courage – the courage to be disciplined, and perhaps ruthless!

I love order and simplicity, yet can create chaos with papers on my desk, until I apply the valuable tip from a friend: Start at one end and deal with each item systematically – do not jump ahead! Over the years I have applied her advice in other ways, including when packing to move, by commencing at one corner and working around each room, listing each item in an indexed notebook.

There are many books of support available. Kathy Paauw at www.orgcoach.net offers a free download covering 7 Strategies to Overcome Overwhelm. Clutter Coach and Feng Shui consultant, Denise Linn has an excellent website at www.deniselinn.com on elemental space clearing.

In order to create space, some key questions to ask are whether an item's purpose serves you well and enriches your life. Is it broken – worth mending? When did you last use it – wear it? Does it have sentimental value? The last one can be the most challenging. As we age, the sifting and sorting become more serious, and a move to a smaller space can mean asking those hard questions, which I recently experienced with a neighbour. My creativity is sleuthing out local thrift stores and, when something comes in, something is donated . . . albeit with reluctance!

So, if overwhelmed, sketch an outline for your desired end result, and then take baby steps: one counter-top, one drawer, 15 - 30 minutes each day. If releasing something that gave you great pleasure is difficult, think about the joy it will give someone else – in essence, you are re-gifting it.

Just as excess doesn't build up overnight, neither does de-cluttering magically happen. Do seek support if that works best for you, or consider trading skills with another. Above all, cut yourself some slack, smile and know you will get through it. Even wise bards of recent centuries, friends Henry Thoreau and Ralph Waldo Emerson, had a sense of humour. Thoreau once stated that the key to living well was to '*simplify, simplify, simplify,*' to which Emerson replied, '*one simplify might have sufficed.*'

I wish you success as you simply simplify your life.

I do not think there is any other quality so essential
to success of any kind as the quality of perseverance.
It overcomes almost everything, even nature.

John D. Rockefeller (1839-1937)

Perseverance . . . Only When I've Done it will I not have to Do It!

Reflecting on your life, are you where you thought you would be today? Or have you reached a turning point and are now in transition? Congratulations, if you answered "yes" to the first question; and "yes" to the second one, as transitions are a positive step, challenging though they can be. Over the years I have had many transitions in career, lifestyle and residence moves, touting that all I wanted was a simple life, yet continuing to create whirlwind and chaotic days. It was desperation 25 years ago that led me to create *Only When,* a whole-life textbook planner assisting readers to turn their dreams into reality. Today's advanced technology makes the written version obsolete, but let's briefly look at each step.

Present Strengths: Your foundation. At an early age
were you creative, tidy, loved animals, gardening, wood-
working? Did some become career building blocks, while
others remain a hobby?

Success Story to Date: Your strengths contributed to your
success story to date – and may have helped identify the
path you decided to take.

Dreams and Ideas: This is the "Wouldn't it be wonderful
if . . ." stage, limited only by desires and imagination. (See
separate chapter, *Are you a Dreamer or a Dream-Maker?*)

Mission or Purpose Statement: A focused statement of the
song you were meant to sing, expressing your values and
serving as a benchmark for assessing whether goals and
intentions are in alignment. A goal has a completion date
whereas a mission can be life enduring.

Highest Priorities: An overview of intentions, with
anticipated dates, both short and long-term.

Commitments (Action): Putting *work clothes* on primary
intentions. This is the "doing" part, without which nothing
can be achieved. "Doing" includes scheduling balance and
quiet reflective times into your day. When I was running
faster and faster on a treadmill, a wise counsellor friend
suggested I pause and reflect before beginning again. I
heeded her excellent advice, which led to reading Trina

Paulus' delightful book, *Hope for the Flowers,* about the life of two caterpillars that struggle, cocoon and emerge as beautiful butterflies . . . after they cocooned!

Added Strengths: These often come about by pushing through comfort zones, depending on our energy and circumstances. Although I've lived outside mine most of my adult life, with the accuracy of 20/20 hindsight, it was stretched too far for too long!

Continuing Success Story: This is the journey that never ends, symbolically represented as an ever-upward spiral, open at the top. As late author and motivational speaker, Zig Ziglar wrote: *You are the only one who can use your ability . . . it is an awesome responsibility.*

I wish you perseverance and continuing success on your journey.

This above all: To thine own self be true.
William Shakespeare (1564-1616)

Let the Real You Step Forward . . . and move from the Shadows into the Sunshine

As research for his book, *The Five Secrets You Must Discover Before You Die,* Dr. John Izzo canvassed 15,000 people aged 59 to 106, asking what it meant to live a meaningful life. He condensed replies to the top five, identifying *Be True to Yourself* as number one. Similarly, it was also the number one regret expressed when CBC Radio Host Tom Allen discussed Bonnie Ware's book, *The Top 5 Regrets of the Dying: I wish I had the courage to live a life true to myself, not the life others expected of me.*

What might stop us from being true to ourselves and our authentic self? Could it be the need to please others, unclear boundaries, living in the shadows, or driven by the opinion of others? As a legacy for his and other young children, knowing his death was imminent, Randy Pausch wrote *The Last Lecture,* a university speech he delivered and expanded into his book, about life's important lessons, and particularly not obsessing over what people thought. Wise words indeed, oftentimes easier said than done.

Answers to the questions above took me many years of searching *hither and yon* before I identified and embraced them. I knew how to 'suit up and show up,' as the occasion demanded, often masquerading an outer bravado that covered up inner insecurity. A harsh moment was when I discovered Charles Finn's poem, *Please Hear What I'm Not Saying,* written in 1966 . . . *"Don't be fooled by me, for I wear a mask . . . I wear a thousand masks . . . and none of them are me."* Its impact has gone around the world and is available online: *https://poetrybycharlescfinn.com*

I have never forgotten a Toastmaster friend's talk, *The Head is a Lousy Hunter*, about his relentless search for answers far and wide, only to discover many years later that his *golden grail* was located twelve inches from his head, in his heart. The journey from one's head to one's heart doesn't happen all at once . . . *you become (real),* said the wise Skin Horse to the lovable Rabbit in Margery Williams 1922 favourite, *The Velveteen Rabbit.*

It is often a process that commences with the intuitive awareness of being off balance, and then hearing and heeding the gentle whispers of our inner voice, or – more harshly in my case – owning the truth when reading Finn's poem! It is a journey worth taking, for it can lead us out of the shadows and into the sunshine.

Reflecting on your important life lessons, what advice would you share with another?

To a young heart everything is fun.
Charles Dickens (1812-1870)

Young at Heart on the Journey from Aging to Saging

Do you find that as you age chronologically, your definition of *older* also expands? I do! A continuing fascination with people doing amazing things in their later years led to research for my MBA paper in Metaphysics, and the discovery of a love letter project, which I share below for *your* consideration.

With limited thinking in my early 20s I believed I would be *settled in my ways* by or before age 30 – until a friend of 35 returned to Ireland and opened a hardware store . . . and opened *my* eyes! In my mid-30s I met a lady who became a lawyer at 65. Over the years my thinking continued to expand with numerous residence moves, marrying my partner at 49, starting a new corporate venture at 56, qualifying as a minister at 66, and completing degree courses at 76. Could my 20-year-old self have imagined this? With incredulity, if at all!

The television program guide of British Columbia's *Knowledge Network* recently carried a story titled, *One Red Hot Grandma.* It was about a lady who believed in getting the most out of each day, thinking outside the box, and being open to learning new things, which she felt kept her going. At 86 she won the key role in a popular television commercial, and had a lot of fun doing it. It seems this lady applied the sage wisdom of Oliver Wendell Holmes, that old age was 15 years older than she was!

With our expanding lifetime expectancy, continuing research is being done by organizations, care and leisure centres, to provide a quality lifestyle for people as they age. However, regardless of how much is offered, it is still up to each of us, within our present circumstances, to avail ourselves of opportunities, and hopefully have fun as we do. A special friend, then in her 90s, enjoyed wearing her nursery rhyme *Old Mother Hubbard* hat as she gave out Christmas gifts.

Your Second Fifty: Rising above the Fears of Aging, is an inspiring documentary film produced by Laurent Goldstein, based on Frank Moffat's book of the same name. It has two brilliant suggestions: Consider that your second fifty is the best time of your life; and start working on your 100th birthday speech!

So let's go forward with a young heart as we continue our journey, live our life laced with fun, and start drafting our 100th birthday speech. To borrow words from Mother Teresa, it would be our love letter to the world!

Nature is never static, it is always changing . . .
Kilroy J. Oldster, Author

Seasons of our Lives

Do you see yourself in a certain Season? Do you believe that where you are on your journey is your perfect age? People come into our lives, journey with us for a certain time, then may leave to take another path, yet ours continues, and evolves. I share with you the result of an assignment that illustrates my belief. At the time, now over thirty years ago, I could not have known that it would become a metaphor for my life. It was part of a weekend retreat in the mountains, appropriately named *The Wall*, as its purpose was to break through any stuck areas in our lives. Our assignment was to connect with something in Nature, write about it and then share with the group. Looking around, anxious for *any* idea, I noticed some tiny red shoots at the base of a tall cedar tree, and wrote the following:

> *I had my beginning when an eagle flew overhead many years ago. The seed it dropped fell close to a tall cedar tree. I squirreled into the ground and lay quietly until spring. And I dreamed many dreams. It was a cold snowy winter. I didn't know that I was*

being protected by the cedar tree from the harshest of winds.

In that first spring I broke through the ground and looked around me. I wasn't very tall, but I saw I was different from my neighboring cedar. As spring moved into summer, my leaves grew; they were a different shape from the other trees around me. As the weather turned cooler they changed colours, and when the frost came, one by one they dropped to the ground. I watched, and I wondered.

Each year I had more branches, more leaves. Some of my fallen leaves remained close by, while others danced – rising up with the wind, whirling into a spiral, before taking off again, headed for new destinations.

So the years went by. I matured, I grew. Intuitively I was connected to each leaf that had ever been a part of me. I 'felt' their ups and downs, their ecstasy as they soared, and their peace when they fell. They were free spirits on their own mission. I had given them birth.

Many times I wondered what my purpose was. In my early years I was a tiny sapling at the base of my cedar and often wished I was a tall giant in the forest. But now that I am mature I no longer wish to be other than myself. I have accepted that I am different; I

*like my red leaves that stand out and are noticed.
And I do have a special purpose: my leaves that fall
to the ground when the frost comes, nurture not only
my roots but those of my cedar, so we continue our
journey of preparing for the following spring, for
another new beginning.*

*We are different, my cedar and I, but we are one – just
as I am not only one with every leaf that was ever
a part of me, but I am one with all of Nature. I still
dream many dreams. My journey is one of exploration
– of growing, learning, accepting myself, and sending
my leaves out into the universe to nurture new life. It
is a journey that will never end. In my own way I soar
like the eagle that gave me life.*

— Dorothy Blandford, Oct. 1984 (Snowqualmie, WA).

Relating that experience to the seasons of my life, I was
then in my summer, which was a pendulum of peaks and
valleys. My spring had been a time of dreaming, continuous
learning and creating new foundations. Now, in my late
autumn, my evolving journey has continued as a harvest of
learning, albeit many experiences brilliantly disguised as
'oops' roads, which I define as: "seemed a good idea at the
time; do not repeat." If you have had similar experiences,
don't be discouraged; I read that if Plan A doesn't work,
there are 25 more letters!

Nature is a wonderful teacher, flowing from one season to the next, as if passing on the baton, but is never static. Let us also be in that flow by staying young at heart during each season while maintaining a childlike curiosity. One way to do this is by bridging the generation gap, for we can learn so much from young people, and they from us. When doing extensive research for my thesis on *Aging to Saging,* I talked to many elders: one 90-year-old said he received a lot of happiness from young people as he was always learning something new; similarly another, at 83, said he found younger people stimulating and made a point of staying in touch with them.

Like Nature, let's not remain static, but be a student of life throughout our seasons, sharing our stories. We know, as Irish singer *Enja* reminds us in her song *Pilgrim*, we can't change what's over, but only where we go. And, from an anonymous author: *Age is merely the number of years the world has been enjoying you.* And so it has!

Every step is an end,
and every step is a fresh beginning.
Johann Wolfgang von Goethe (1749-1832)

Stepping Stones — From Despair to Happiness and Inner Peace, and on to Joy

This is a condensed version of *Stepping Stones* that was written in 2006 as support through life's changes, such as the loss of a significant person, pet, job, or independence. It is based on my personal path as a Minister of Compassionate Care, a life with many hills and valleys, the loss of my partner of 35 years, and my last corporate role of supporting those in career transition.

The original booklet had five steps. Due to continuing studies and reflection, I have now added an additional step, *Joy.* You may decide to first read it through from beginning to end, and then go back more slowly, step by step, capturing thoughts and ideas in a notebook as you read. If you are in the midst of change and your world isn't peaceful right now, let's make this journey together, and go to our first Stepping Stone, *Hope.*

Hope . . . or even a glimpse of Hope

Hope is a safe harbor in which we can find refuge when the storms of life roughly toss us around.
The Woman's Book of Spirit: Meditation
for the Thirsty Soul.

*I*f you're moving from a fog of despair onto this Stepping Stone, it's like shedding light into the darkness. It's putting your feet on a path that your eyes can't even see. When I was very young I would walk with my father down a dark country road to my grandmother's home, gripping tightly to his hand, fearful of tripping. He would tell me that my eyes would adjust, and when they did, I'd see a glimpse of the road. In a similar way, I see that moving out of a fog into light, is a glimpse of Hope.

An important part of healing is identifying feelings. Are you:

Sad, because you don't feel you can go on due to a loss or change in circumstances?

Worried whether you will have sufficient funds to meet your monthly expenses?

Tearful, have low energy, feel lonely?

In your notebook, make three headings across the top of the page, as illustrated:

I am feeling	I feel this way because	I really want to feel
Sad		
Tearful		
Frustrated		
Angry		

The third column, *I really want to feel*, is a section you can return to as more insights occur. For now, look at one aspect of how you would like to feel, and what one small step you might take that would give you a glimpse of hope, or feel like a safe harbour. Even a tiny step can make a *huge* difference and be the catalyst for creating a new beginning. Dr. Martin Seligman, known as the Father of Positive

Psychology, wrote that life can be brutal, but if we always have options we will always have hope.

One such option might be writing a daily journal of your thoughts and feelings, for your eyes alone, unless you choose to share it. A friend commenced daily journal writing following the death of his wife, and continued for years; another wrote and published a book, based on his journaling. Going for a walk at your favourite location, or asking a friend to join you for coffee, are positive steps. What one thing will you do today to move you forward? In the words of Elizabeth Barrett Browning, you will be lighting tomorrow with today.

Faith

Faith is the bird that feels the light and sings while the dawn is still dark.
Rabindranath Tagore (1861–1941)

We have moved from our first Stepping Stone of Hope to our next one of Faith. Oprah Winfrey linked these together when she said: *Where's there's Hope there's Faith, and Faith creates miracles.* Having faith is akin to believing in something, which makes it stronger than hope.

For example:

We believe that morning will follow night.
We believe if we plant daffodils, they appear as daffodils.
Although we do not see electricity, we believe that the light will come on when we flick the switch.

Scientifically, there are reasons. Personally, I see these as wonderful miracles, in which I have complete faith. Would you agree that faith need neither be a certainty nor a conviction – perhaps not even logical, but is a belief? What do you believe to be true and have faith in?

Dan Millman, author of *Sacred Journey of the Peaceful Warrior,* wrote: *Faith is the courage to live your life as if everything that happens does so for your highest good and learning.* However, if your heart is broken and shattered into a million pieces, it may be a stretch to accept that idea. We do not easily get over a loss or the circumstances that changed our lives, but the grief does gentle and soften in time. For now, have confidence that you have special gifts and inner resources to draw upon. A church billboard carried the message: *Faith is not a step into the dark, but is a leap into the light,* similar to our first Stepping Stone that shed light onto our path.

Being active is one component of what faith is. Active, yes, but it need not be a solo act. My invaluable support is a heart-centered spiritual coach who listens as I 'think aloud,' leading to uncovering buried ideas. Before moving to our third Stepping Stone, please capture highlights of your natural strengths, listing 1, 2 or 3 things you have faith that you will do. And, acknowledge yourself for bravery!

Surrender ... Finding the Simple Way

The ability to surrender is a sign of spiritual maturity . . . life gets easier.
Cheryl Richardson, *The Unmistakable Touch of Grace*

What comes to your mind when you think of the word "surrender"? Giving up? Letting go? It can be detaching and trusting in an outcome, without clearly seeing the end result, or making life simpler by releasing heavy weights. Are you putting weights on your shoulders that could be lifted? Are you driven by the 'shoulds' of others? In the words of the famous philosopher, Abraham Maslow: *There is a time to become independent of the good opinion of others.*

On my bedroom wall, in a framed needlepoint by a friend, are words I awake to each morning: *Do your best, leave the rest. Angels do no more.* Good advice indeed for those of us who like to handle every tiny detail, and especially those of us who are over-achievers.

Before continuing, capture in your notebook what you would be willing to release, knowing the road ahead would be easier. Include any limiting beliefs around what you think you must or should do, or who you feel you are. Take a moment to look back at your natural strengths that you listed in the previous section on Faith, for these are reminders of the real you.

Did identifying some of those weights help you to feel lighter? Did they let in the truth of how strong you really are? Cheryl Richardson, in her insightful book, *The Unmistakable Touch of Grace*, wrote that Surrender is the key that unlocks the door to Grace . . . so let's continue our journey and move to our fourth Stepping Stone, *Grace*.

Grace

Grace comes into the soul, as the morning sun into the world: first a dawning, then a light, and at last the sun in his full and excellent brightness.
Thomas Adams (1818–1905)

Grace is our fourth stepping stone. What *is* Grace? It's a small word, with many applications, as well as extensive Biblical references: We grace someone with our presence, enter a room with grace, and say grace before a meal. I believe that it is also self-acceptance, being in the flow, having a sense of ease, and a place where we can go in our minds to take us out of anxiety.

How would you define Grace, when you feel at ease and in the flow of life? Is it when you garden, sit in silence, golf, build something, sew, knit, walk, listen to music, or read? A gentleman, participating in my Hospice grief support group after the death of his wife, shared that a lady at his care home was teaching him to knit, how he enjoyed learning something new and was experiencing a new-found sense of calm. Sitting on a log at the beach is what I call my "sit and stare" time. At home, listening to music is restorative, from classical to country to gospel, to sentimental Irish Celtic. At other times, brushing my cat's long coat, or reading aloud to her – how much she absorbs is debatable, but she purrs happily. Another new peaceful endeavour is bringing life to images in a colouring book.

Perhaps you might prefer something more active, like running, dancing, swimming, or attempting a new project. A friend, wracked with grief due to her husband's recent death, took an active role out of necessity. Discovering some urgent renovations needed for her home, she found a retired contractor willing to help and, in working with him not only learned valuable new skills, but reduced expenses considerably. Another friend built a doll's house with meticulous detail. When he entered into a solid new relationship he happily sold it, but building it drew on his creative side and alleviated his sadness.

Grief and its suffering may be inevitable during our lifetime, but how we respond is a personal decision. Before continuing, identify how and when you experience Grace, and feel peaceful.

Happiness and Inner Peace

Happiness never decreases by being shared.
Buddha.

We have journeyed from the depth of despair to Hope, on to Faith, created space by Surrendering, and gently glided into Grace. The fifth step, Happiness and Inner Peace, I have braided together, as when we have inner peace, we feel happy, and when we are happy, we have inner peace.

Inner peace may be elusive during challenging times. Grief, especially, is something we can't get around, but only go through. Tears are healing . . . although you may be wondering, as I certainly did, how one body can hold so much water. During times of anxiety the following Buddhist practice can help create a sense of peace: *Breathing in, I calm my body; breathing out, I smile.* And, a smile relaxes hundreds of facial muscles!

Although we have moved sequentially through these steps, realistically that may not be the case. Sometimes life is a roller-coaster of highs and lows, where one day might feel like being in the midst of a raging storm, often with a frenzied rush into the urgent, and the next an oasis of calm. I find pre-planning for the next day, including wardrobe, leads to a calmer start.

Do you keep a Daily Gratitude Journal of special moments, such as seeing a beautiful sunrise or sunset, hearing a bird singing, meeting with a friend, or noticing a brave flower pushing through a crack in the sidewalk? Expressing appreciation carries us a long way towards happiness, and reviewing those moments, especially on a grey day, can lift our spirits.

When experiencing happiness and peace in your heart, you are blessing yourself and those around you. A *blessing is a circle of light drawn around a person to protect, heal and strengthen*, wrote John O'Donohue in his book, *Blessings*. As you go about your day, pause at times to feel that circle of light protecting, healing and strengthening *you*.

As I have added a sixth stepping stone to the original version, let's now go on to *Joy*.

Joy

Joy is not in things, it is in us.
Richard Wagner, German Composer (1813-1883)

Joy, our next stepping stone, creates a personal feeling for each of us. With the illustration above I share *my* lifetime and continuing joy, which always bring an inner warmth – the snowdrops! Why? They inspire me by symbolizing hope and courage, despite their fragility, and are the first to push through the winter ground and snow early in the New Year. Growing up in Belfast, they were my first purchase each January from the flower ladies sitting at the City Hall – then at sixpence a bunch! When do you feel *joy*? Can you define it?

During a trip to Ireland, a short time after having written the original *Stepping Stones,* I asked a long-time friend if he was happy. *I'm content,* he answered, adding that *joy* was more significant to him. Four years later, in 2010, subsequent to extensive research, I wrote my doctoral thesis on words I heard as I awoke – *Happiness, The New Now,* later adding, *An Inside-Out Affair.* I believe those words also apply to our sixth stepping stone of *Joy,* echoing the words of Richard Wagner, that it is not in things but is in us, and I suggest, more tranquil. Each moment is new and each one is now, and a feeling of joy is indeed an *inside-out affair!*

Over the intervening eight years, many *joy* references have been presented, including *The Book of Joy,* with discussions between His Holiness the Dalai Lama and Archbishop Desmond Tutu. In the introduction Archbishop Tutu felt that joy was much bigger than happiness, as it was not dependent on external circumstances, whereas happiness often was. Mary C. Neal, MD, who had a near death experience when her kayak overturned and plunged over a steep waterfall, also felt that joy and happiness were different things, with joy transcending everything. (*7 Lessons from Heaven).*

In the midst of writing this segment I had a visit with an Ontario friend who came west to see her parents. Happiness was what I felt as I anticipated our time together, but the two hours that we shared were absolute joy. So my definition of *joy* is not easily defined in words, but one that passes all understanding, from the inside-out. How would you define *joy?* Do you feel that it transcends *happiness?*

As you go through each segment of *Stepping Stones* to arrive at Happiness, Inner Peace and on to Joy, know that each step is a personal journey and learning experience in which Hope, or a glimpse of it, always resides, and so the circle is unbroken. You have very special gifts that only you can share with the world . . . and the world wants, and needs your gifts!

I wish you peace, happiness, joy and rich blessings as you continue your journey.

Blessèd be!

*I long to accomplish a great and noble task, but
it is my chief duty to accomplish humble tasks
as though they were great and noble.*

Helen Keller (1880-1968)

On Making a Difference

Do you, as I do at times, question whether you are being enough, doing enough, accomplishing enough? What if what we are doing is enough? What if we gave ourselves a break and instead of setting our standards on completing herculean tasks, we honoured ourselves for the smallest of tasks, seeing each one as *great and noble* with cumulative value beyond measure? A perfect example of making a difference one-by-one is the often told starfish story, part of an essay by Loren Eiseley (1907-1977).

It tells of an older man walking along a beach that was littered with thousands of starfish that had been washed ashore by the high tide. As he walked he came upon a young boy who was eagerly throwing the starfish back into the ocean, one-by-one. Puzzled, he asked the boy what he was doing. The boy's simple answer was: *I'm saving these starfish, sir.* The man replied: S*on, there are thousands of starfish and only one of you, what difference can you make?*

The boy picked up a starfish, gently tossed it into the water and turning to the man said: *I made a difference to that one!*

The above is an example, in its simplicity, of a young person making a difference. Yet, we each know people of all ages, from pre-teens to those in their nineties and beyond, who are inspiring us by who they are and what they do, through their messages, their music and other mediums. At times a *great and noble* task may be stepping back, taking time out to reflect, before barreling down the next path. It may be seizing an opportunity in the moment – smiling at a passer-by, giving tourist directions, holding a door open, or sending energy to someone.

Years ago, I was the recipient of acknowledgment on how we can make a difference by sending 'comfort vibes' to another. The host at a packed University of Victoria auditorium advised that the evening's well-known speaker was delayed by traffic. On arrival he came immediately to the podium, apologized and commenced speaking. While listening, I intuitively sent him some 'calming energy,' knowing how anxious I could have been in those circumstances. After the presentation, happening to join a group speaking with him, he looked over and said: *Aah, the lady with the kind eyes.* That happened years ago, but the importance of the energy of the thoughts we extend to another was a valuable never-forgotten lesson.

The late Fred Rogers (1928-2003), was a special man who made a difference just by being who he was, and teaching children to be kind as the host of *Mister Rogers Neighborhood.* His small book, *Life's Journeys according to Mister Rogers,* is a collection of short inspirational thoughts containing many examples of humble tasks that are *great and noble.*

*To know what you prefer instead of humbly
saying 'amen' to what the world tells you,
is to keep your soul alive.*

Robert Louis Stevenson (1850-1894)

Bedtime Stories and Colouring Books

*D*o you recall when someone last read you a bedtime story? While attending a recent ministry conference I was reminded by one of the speakers of the value of colouring. This triggered a distant memory of a meaningful bedtime story read by a friend during an overnight stay, which created a gigantic shift in *my* thinking! The story was *Paint Me a Masterpiece,* Chapter 24 of *Orbiting the Giant Hairball,* by Gordon MacKenzie, a cartoonist, and writer formerly with the Vancouver Sun and Hallmark Cards. I share with you a shortened version of this parable.

Personalizing the story, God outlines the exhausting journey I would take in the process of being born, shows me an artist's canvas and asks if I would paint Him a Masterpiece. I agreed. All goes according to plan, except that upon my arrival the big people – adults – see the pristine canvas and take it away for safe-keeping. When they give it back years later it contains lines and numbers, and a message that I am to paint within the lines, and follow the numbers in sequence. The implication was that if I followed the rules and worked hard, my life would be a Masterpiece.

Later, reflecting on the story and my life's *Masterpiece,* I realized, like the author, that it wasn't mine at all, but was made up of what I *thought* I should do, or believed was the *responsible* thing to do. For sixty years I had, more or less, followed the rules (of others), worked hard, and occasionally – with great daring – coloured outside the lines, often resulting in new beginnings that took me back inside the lines. It was time to pay heed to those wise words of Robert Louis Stevenson, and know what I preferred.

MacKenzie's book is a creative masterpiece of words and colourful illustrations. He ends his story with the reminder that we each have a Masterpiece inside us, one unlike any that has ever been created, or ever will be, and that if we go to our grave without painting it, it will not get done, for there is no one else who can create it.

That story was read to me fifteen years ago, but its impact has never been forgotten. Two years ago a friend gifted me with my first colouring book of mandalas, each with an inspirational quotation. Slowly, randomly selecting coloured pencils on a whim, it was completed – and yes, at times I did colour outside the lines! In addition to being an enjoyable new experience, it was also a meditative one, as my mind went to a still place when I coloured, creating a peaceful ending to my day.

Wherever you are in your life, consider it as a metaphor and ask: *Is this my Masterpiece?* I wish you happy colouring, or endeavour of your choice; and that you and a friend might share a meaningful story, at bedtime, or at any time.

Appreciation can make a day, even change a life.
Your willingness to put it all into words is all
that is necessary.

Margaret Cousins (1878-1954)

Handwritten Thank-You Notes

Today there are many ways in which we can express gratitude, but sending a handwritten thank-you note or card has value beyond measure.

Writing a sincere brief note of appreciation following a job interview is (I feel) essential, and could give you, the interviewee, a slight edge. At the very least the interviewer would see it as a courteous gesture. In the case of a panel or multiple interviews, a note should be personally addressed to each. A Google search gives excellent examples, stressing the importance of legible handwriting, and proofing for accuracy. The interview may be over, but your *thank-you* note will be included with your file!

I acknowledge I was raised on the importance of writing letters, especially to relatives overseas, and then subsequently to my parents and friends once I immigrated to Canada. Costly long-distance calls were only made on special occasions, or for emergencies. Today's technology makes communication much easier with excellent long-distance rates, emails and video viewing. Yes, it still needs a personal commitment to write a letter or card, make a phone call or send an email – and, very possibly, your gift will brighten that person's day!

It is a delight to find a personal letter in my mailbox, so I hope that it never becomes an archaic gesture that loses its significance. Who is on your list? What you say doesn't have to be wordy. A card with *thinking about you* tells your recipient that you care and appreciate them.

As this is the last chapter of these whimsical thoughts and ideas, it is fitting that I close with *my* gratitude and appreciation for you, Dear Reader, and thank you for *your* interest!

Let's keep writing, shall we?

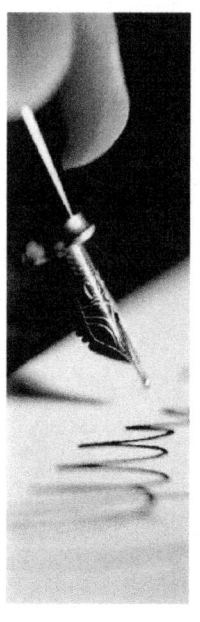

Some last thoughts . . .

Often I wondered if *Into the Mystic* would ever come together, as hundreds of hours led to each tale being written and edited many times, target dates arriving, passing by, and new ones being set. Now, on this date of the 58th anniversary of arriving in Canada from Northern Ireland on my first airplane ride, I give it wings and release it to go out into the world with a life of its own, finding its way to those for whom it has a message of hope and encouragement. It is based on my life experiences and was written with divine guidance and inspiration from people who impacted my life over decades, both living and dead.

Thank you for joining me by our fireside. I trust that some of the ideas within these pages will be a thread of support on the colourful tapestry of *your* life. I have not lived a *conventional* life, but an amazing one and, in the words on the bronze plaque above my computer by 84-year-old Michelangelo, *I am still learning*. I wish the same for you, for it's the best way to stay young at heart!

It is my joy to have shared these thoughts with you. If I can support you on *your* amazing journey, I would be honoured.

Blessèd be . . .

Dorothy

South Surrey, B.C.
June 28, 2018

We read to know we are not alone.

C.S. Lewis (1898-1963)

My Special Reading

Anam Cara: A Book of Celtic Wisdom (1997) – *John O'Donohue*

The Book of Joy . . . Lasting Happiness in a Changing World (2016)
– *His Holiness the Dalai Lama & Archbishop Desmond Tutu*

The Five Secrets You Must Discover Before You Die (2008)
– *Dr. John Izzo*

The Four Agreements . . . A Practical Guide to Personal Freedom
(1997) – *Don Miguel Ruiz*

The Gifts of Imperfection . . . Let go of who you think you're
supposed to be and embrace who you are (2010) – *Brené Brown*

Hope for the Flowers . . . A tale about hope for adults and
caterpillars who can read (1972) – *Trina Paulus*

Life's Journeys according to Mister Rogers . . . Things to
Remember Along the Way (2005) – *Fred Rogers*

Orbiting the Giant Hairball (1996) – *Gordon MacKenzie*

The Tao of Pooh (1982) – *Benjamin Hoff*

Tuesdays with Morrie (1997) – *Mitch Albom*

The Velveteen Rabbit (first published 1922) – *Margery Williams*

You Had To Be There (1997) – *Robert Collins*

By way of total disclosure, my *time out of time* bedtime favourite
is an often-read romance novel by Nora Roberts!

About the Author

Who *is* this Rev. Dr. Dorothy Blandford?

By reading these tales we do get *some* glimpses.

Obviously, *retirement* isn't in her DNA!

She believes she may be missing a *moderation* gene.

Lives by her own mythical definition of *normal*!

Agrees her 3-legged cat, Cadi, is her confidante . . . and is the soul of discretion!

How *she* sums up her life: *"I did THAT?. . . WOW!!!"* Or: *"I did THAT? . . . What WAS I thinking!!!"*

Dr. Dorothy can be contacted through her website at www.innisfreespirit.com or by e-mail at info@innisfreespirit.com

Made in the USA
Columbia, SC
17 September 2018